Total Rewa

Paul Thompson

The Chartered Institute of Personnel and Development is the leading publisher of books and reports for personnel and training professionals, students, and all those concerned with the effective management and development of people at work. For full details of all our titles, please contact the Publishing Department:

Tel: 020 8263 3387
Fax: 020 8263 3850

E-mail: publish@cipd.co.uk

To view and purchase all CIPD titles:
www.cipd.co.uk/bookstore

Total Reward

Paul Thompson

Paul Thompson is co-founder, with Michael Armstrong, and managing partner of the reward management website, www.e-reward.co.uk

First published 2002

Cover design by Curve
Designed by Beacon GDT
Typeset by Paperweight
Printed in Great Britain by Short Run Press

British Library Cataloguing in Publication Data
A catalogue record for this book is available from the British Library

ISBN 0 85292 975 7

Chartered Institute of Personnel and Development,
CIPD House, Camp Road, London SW19 4UX

Tel: 020 8971 9000
Fax: 020 8263 3333
Website: www.cipd.co.uk

Incorporated by Royal Charter. Registered charity no. 1079797.

Executive summary

◻ It is becoming increasingly recognised that in order to differentiate one's organisation from others in the jobs market it is necessary to offer more than just a good salary and pension. In an era of skills shortages, potential recruits and existing employees are becoming more sophisticated in seeking a more congenial work-life balance.

◻ In a climate of full employment, a shortage of workers with key skills, and a more mobile workforce, employers have to ensure that they 'stand out from the crowd' to be seen as the employer of choice.

◻ The past few years have seen an increase in the development of total reward programmes by benefits consultants. It is clear that each organisation needs a tailor-made system to address its particular needs, and that a one-size-fits-all approach will not succeed.

◻ The benefits that flow from a total reward scheme are: easier recruitment of better-quality staff; reduced wastage from staff turnover; better business performance; and an enhanced reputation of the organisation as an 'employer of choice'.

◻ The 'psychological contract' between employers and employees requires that there be trust on both sides. The provision of a total reward scheme demonstrates that the employer takes into consideration the needs of the individual employee and is prepared to be flexible in meeting those needs. The employee also feels to some extent in control by being able to select various options from a range of benefits.

◻ So far, few employers have made the switch from a traditional pay scheme to a total reward system, largely because of the daunting task of making such a wholesale change. The few organisations that have made the change have done so mainly because of outside pressures – for example, to harmonise benefits following a merger or take-over.

◻ The 'cafeteria' approach to benefits is greatly appreciated by staff, because each employee can select the mix of pay, benefits in kind, and flexible time, that best suits his/her particular circumstances. In return, the employer has a more contented, stable, happier and productive workforce.

◘ Organisations that have successfully made the transition, such as FSA and AstraZeneca, have reported wholly beneficial results from doing so. The effort of changing may be great, but the benefits are even greater.

1 | Introduction

Creating a fun, challenging, and empowered work environment in which individuals are able to use their abilities to do meaningful jobs for which they are shown appreciation is likely to be a more certain way to enhance motivation and performance – even though creating such an environment may be more difficult and take more time than merely turning the reward lever.

Jeffrey Pfeffer (1998a)

There was a time when an organisation's reward package was a pretty straightforward thing. But the era in which reward was just about cash and benefits is gone for ever; increasingly the emphasis in leading organisations is on a total reward approach, including more intangible rewards like the work environment and quality of life considerations, the opportunity for advancement and recognition, and flexible working – everything from telecommuting to variable hours. Some of the most renowned reward experts on both sides of the Atlantic urge us to view reward more holistically, and they reckon the evolution towards a total reward approach has truly begun.

The essential idea is that we need to rethink what is and what is not reward. Your reward strategy needs to encompass all aspects of reward if it is to add real value, enhance employee commitment and minimise the loss of your best people – and their intellectual capital and knowledge-based skills. To do this, organisations first need to understand what their key employees value in order to feel motivated and engaged. In short, total reward is a hybrid approach to reward management which seeks to match the needs of the company with those of its employees.

> *'...we need to rethink what is and what is not reward.'*

Total reward helps organisations pursue a wide range of managerial objectives

With an increasingly competitive world market, it has never been more vital for employers to know that they are maximising the capabilities of their employees. Major organisations – indeed any employer vying for the most productive staff – are having to look at ever more imaginative ways to communicate what it is about working for them that is so special and different. They are putting together increasingly sophisticated total reward packages in a bid to hold on to their most valued staff.

Reward practices in organisations like AstraZeneca, Cisco, Financial Services Authority, IBM, Royal Bank of Scotland, a host of professional service firms and others, are undergoing major change – which reflect a fundamental acceptance of the importance of people to business success. These businesses are taking a broader total reward approach that seeks to reinforce desired employee behaviour and actions and at the same time creates a compelling value proposition.

The appeal of total reward lies in its perceived ability to further an array of organisational goals. It's supposed to be the answer to employers' seemingly endless quest for a solution to the 'holy trinity' of traditional pay goals: recruitment, retention and motivation. Then, and much more innovatively, there is also a batch of managerial objectives linked with organisational transformation.

Total reward is seen by its proponents as a very powerful tool for stimulating or reinforcing organisational or cultural change by sending the right signals to employees about corporate values and beliefs while delivering an excellent return on your organisation's investment. What's more, it's potentially pretty potent in assisting employers to align their human resource and business strategies with employee needs in order to improve performance.

While the optimum mix differs widely from company to company, the objective of a well-designed total reward programme is to:

- enhance recruitment and retention

- drive desired behaviour in your workforce

- reinforce your business strategy

- ensure long-term competitive advantage.

The pressures for change

We have witnessed a profound economic transformation over the past few decades, which has had far-reaching implications for the way that we work and do business, and has led to the emergence of a truly global economy. Demographic shifts, such as the increasing number of women in the workforce, skill shortages, coupled with new economic forces – such as global competition, a flood of mergers and acquisitions, technological improvements, dot-com mania – have fundamentally changed the employment landscape.

Much of the business community is now looking for entirely new ways to work smarter, faster and more efficiently. Doing a job as it was done before is no longer enough. This means winning – and, crucially, sustaining – employees' commitment to new ways of working.

For management consultants Hay Group, leading-edge organisations are increasingly looking for 'transformational solutions' in the way they recognise, recruit, reward and retain their people (Murlis and Watson, 2001).

They want and need to make step changes in their performance year on year to meet the competitive demands of the global marketplace. In most cases, these changes in performance can only come through people. The best of these organisations therefore seek to move forward on the basis of a sound understanding of what it is their employees need in the package on offer to feel well rewarded and motivated.

Reasons why organisations adopt total reward

As Chapters 4 to 7 illustrate, the literature suggests that the evolution to a total reward approach stems from a wide range of factors, including:

People are a critical source of competitive advantage

The twenty-first century has brought companies squarely into a business world where people can make or break an organisation, forcing companies to recognise that the strategies that once brought them success may no longer deliver high performance. We are told that our most important assets, knowledge and talent, are at a premium and the global 'war for talent' is a serious issue for business.

 HR professionals simply cannot afford to remain trapped in the ways of doing things as in the past – the reward management landscape must be transformed.

Workforces are becoming ever more diverse

Several demographic and social changes now combine to make the argument for a total reward perspective even more pressing. Workforces are far from homogeneous: the trend is towards an ever-ageing population, a high proportion of women in full-time employment and a dramatic increase in lone parents and carers of elderly people. More employees have responsibilities outside the workplace – and a pressing imperative to balance those responsibilities with their working lives.

Quite simply, the workplace has altered dramatically over the past 30 years or so and old reward methods are no longer appropriate as employers accept that their most valuable asset is their workforce.

Employees want greater work-life balance

A flood of recent studies shows that today's workers are looking for better ways to balance work and leisure, family and community time. Their values are shifting. Individuals have unique needs that employers are recognising in creating new and innovative total reward programmes. An increasing number of companies have come to realise that they need to develop practices and policies that facilitate a work-life balance. The move away from traditional nine-to-five work culture has made employees ever more aware of the options for when and where they work.

Companies are increasingly keen to accommodate requirements arising from their employees' domestic responsibilities

Money is not the only motivator

The role of money as a motivator has been a reward battleground for many years. In truth, organisations seldom think about what sort of things employees really need to feel motivated. All too often line management and top management persist in relying predominantly on financial rewards (the so-called 'extrinsic' factors), assuming they will coincide with whatever it is that motivates their staff.

They are neglecting the 'intrinsic' factors, the more powerful levers for motivating and retaining employees – take, for example, job security, job satisfaction, intellectual stimulation and career development. And recognition and opportunities for achievement are essential – albeit underused – motivational techniques.

A basic tenet underpinning the concept of total reward is that sacred managerial pursuits such as improving commitment, encouraging better performance and generating a culture of innovation can rarely be achieved through cash alone.

Employers are more aware of the need to address all aspects of the psychological contract

Proponents of the total reward approach call for a better understanding of why people at work behave in the way they do. They urge us to shift the focus of rewards away from the pay and benefits arena into non-financial rewards. Although introducing incentive pay systems is very much in vogue in the UK, the development of a positive psychological contract would best be served by a more holistic reward regime that seeks to embrace a wider range of initiatives than just pay and benefits. Pay alone cannot reach and motivate all employees. It cannot create the common mindset among the workforce required to open an employee to contributing the discretionary insights and skills necessary to create competitive advantage. There is little doubt that part of the 'glue' binding the employer and employee is psychological.

Employers need to develop an integrated approach to reward

One of the cardinal rules of reward is that the reward system should be 'vertically aligned' – it is supposed to support an organisation's strategy and core values. A key theme that shines through in the literature on total reward is the need for 'horizontal fit' between all of the pay and reward policies with each other and with other HR policies. This ensures, we are told, an aligned HR strategy delivering a consistent message to employees about what is needed for the business to succeed and the HR approach supporting this. That way, no reward innovations take place and no practices are changed without considering how they relate to other aspects of human resource management so that they become mutually supportive.

So, the essence of this new thinking is that a systematic approach which formally integrates all aspects of the employment deal into a total reward package contributes to increases in motivation, higher levels of commitment and improved performance.

Attractions of total reward

What, then, do organisations hope to achieve by embracing total reward strategies? Chapter 8 investigates the benefits that businesses gain from taking a strategic approach to managing their total reward programme.

The arguments for can be summarised under five interlinked headings:

Improved recruitment and retention

The way that organisations value their 'human capital', we are told, is clearly a factor in keeping the right people on board. And the workplace that you create reflects that value, giving you the edge in the battle for scarce talent. Tailoring the total reward package to meet individual needs may be the most effective way of responding to recruitment and retention difficulties.

Heightened visibility in a tight labour market

Some leading companies are using a distinctive array of total reward programmes to build what they call a powerful 'employer brand', which is much more difficult for competitors to copy. By assembling and marketing a compelling reward package that will attract, engage and retain the people needed for organisational success, a good HR brand, it is said, can position a company as an 'employer of choice' and create a competitive advantage. Pay alone cannot create and sustain sufficient competitive advantage or reach and motivate all employees.

Increased flexibility

Stopping your high-fliers, or indeed the 'engine room' of reliable people that organisations depend on, deserting requires a lot more than 'one-size-fits-all' reward programmes. Employers are increasingly looking to customise their total reward packages to give them the edge in attracting and retaining valued employees. Adopting a total reward approach is a useful way of offering significant overall choice within your reward strategy, which meets the needs and lifestyles of individual employees.

Cost effectiveness

The received wisdom is that high-performing companies win the recruitment and retention race by offering higher base salaries. In fact, research by HR consultants Towers Perrin discovered that the top companies are more likely to provide the broader reward package that employees today want. They are putting together ever more sophisticated holistic packages in order to hold on to their most talented employees.

Employers are recognising that well-designed total reward programmes that go beyond standard remuneration by embracing the total work experience are highly valued by employees. Not only do they add more value, they are relatively low in cost.

Competitive advantage

The traditional solution to the recruitment and retention dilemma is to 'throw more money at the problem'. But as this tactic is used by all too many organisations, it does not afford competitive advantage and immediately raises costs.

There is a growing realisation that focusing only on the 'transactional' elements – pay and benefits – creates transactional relationships that can be easily copied. The decision about staying with an employer becomes a purely instrumental calculation. If a job opportunity with another organisation provides 'economic gain', then the employee will jump ship. By contrast, so-called 'relational rewards' are much more likely to create and sustain competitive advantage as they make the organisation distinctive.

A final word

Organisations are increasingly using the full range of extrinsic and intrinsic reward tools to appeal to, retain and motivate their ever more diverse and demanding workforce, and are providing their employees with more choice in the mix of their rewards.

Towers Perrin (1999)

- ◘ Monetary rewards, while important, are not the only – or even the main – consideration of today's employee.

- ◘ Employers are increasingly coming to realise that matching or even exceeding, in monetary terms, what competitors are offering is no longer sufficient to attract or retain workers.

2 | Total reward defined

Total reward is an approach to providing a 'package' of reward to employees in ways that optimise employee satisfaction with reward from their work, and which does this such that the employees' contribution to the employer is optimised at an acceptable cost.

Vicky Wright, CIPD Vice-president, Reward and Partner, Ernst & Young, speaking at the CIPD national conference 2001.

On the face of it, the thinking behind the total reward approach is fairly straightforward – and to be honest not entirely novel. Sandra O'Neal, who is a Principal and Director with the HR consultancy Towers Perrin in the USA, was one of the first pay analysts to champion the idea of total reward. In her influential study in 1998 for the then *ACA Journal* (now *WorldatWork Journal*), she made a compelling case for the need for managers to think about reward in its widest sense when linking reward and business strategy.

As O'Neal explained:

Total rewards embraces everything that employees value in the employment relationship. It integrates a number of classic human resources disciplines and adds some not-so-classic ones.

Definitions of total reward typically encompass not only traditional, quantifiable elements like salary, variable pay and benefits, but also more intangible non-cash elements such as scope to achieve and exercise responsibility, career opportunities, learning and development, the intrinsic motivation provided by the work itself and the quality of working life provided by the organisation.

The notion of total reward also describes what organisations can do with their employment offering to encourage employees to apply their efforts and abilities in ways that will help to achieve the organisation's goals as well as satisfying their own individual needs.

Traditional rewards – such as base pay and benefits – remain important fundamentals that companies must get right in order to compete for and retain key talent. But non-financial rewards that focus on the needs of employees for recognition, achievement, responsibility and personal growth are seen as having a deeper and longer-lasting impact on motivation and commitment than transitory financial rewards. As Murlis and Watson (2001) put it:

The monetary values in the reward package still matter, but they are not the only factors.

How then does it differ from the more conventional total remuneration? The essential point to note is that total reward is not so narrowly focused on the financial aspects of reward. The sum of base salary, variable pay, the value of employee benefits, share ownership and pensions constitutes total remuneration. This represents the complete worth of financial rewards to individuals. The concept of total reward broadens the definition of total remuneration to include the total value of employment. So, rather than a narrow pay and benefits focus, a total reward package encompasses every single investment that an organisation makes in its people, and everything its employees value in the employment relationship.

'...a total reward package encompasses every single investment that an organisation makes in its people...'

Above all, a total reward perspective seeks to answer these questions:

- What types of people will help our business thrive?

- How do you create a working environment that not only brings out the best in the top performers and the 'engine room', but also attracts other top talent and encourages them to stay with your organisation?

- Why do employees choose to remain with a particular employer? And why do they leave?

- What factors motivate performance and commitment?

An integrated approach

While the total reward concept is fairly simple to understand, it is very complex in operation because it has wide-reaching implications for approaches to reward management and for cultural change in organisations. In essence, it is an integrated and strategic approach to reward management, designed to help you create an environment that will attract, nurture and retain the brightest employees.

Gaining a competitive edge involves selecting and arranging the mix of reward elements in a way that capitalises on your organisation's uniqueness or, as the Hay Group puts it, your 'organisational personality'. There is no single template!

In truth, it is common for organisations to deal with one or other of the elements that make up the total reward programme in isolation. But because they are reviewed in such a piecemeal fashion, all too often changes are made without considering how they relate to other aspects of human resource management. As a result, initiatives may not be mutually supportive or aligned with corporate goals. And in the worst cases, innovations may even conflict with one another.

As Duncan Brown (2001), Assistant Director General of the CIPD and one of the UK's most renowned reward thinkers, observes:

There is increasingly a temptation – given the range of reward programmes in many organisations and the increasing complexity of employment law and tax regimes – to adopt a narrow focus on single programmes and to make specific, one-off changes and improvements. This should be resisted, and instead a broad, total rewards approach should be adopted.

For its devotees, the strength of this broader and more integrated, strategic perspective lies in the organisational benefits that might be gained from matching the various elements of the reward system over and above the contribution those individual parts might provide.

A strategic approach

A recurring theme in the total reward literature is the strong agenda of business alignment. Clearly, there is more to total rewards than initially meets the eye. Its proponents make a compelling case for total reward to be strategically managed, designed to meet the evolving needs of organisations and the people they employ. Ultimately, the objective then is to structure the total value of employment so that employee contributions support organisational goals.

On the face of it, total reward has much in common with the more traditional reward strategy development. Helen Murlis and Steve Watson (2001) at the Hay Group have done much to popularise the concept in the UK. As they explain:

This model is therefore reward strategy based – focused on engaged performance which aims to capture personal commitment and involvement. It is a strategic model that considers where the 'war for talent' is taking place.

But total reward goes one stage further. According to Murlis and Watson, what distinguishes it, however, is the:

emphasis on building a much deeper understanding of the employee agenda across all elements of reward… Achieving this can be based on interviews, focus groups and/or survey questionnaires designed to assess what the 'elements of engagement' are and where the priorities lie for the main employee groups in each organisation.

The incidence of total reward programmes

It is difficult to estimate just how many UK organisations have adopted a total reward approach – after all, this broadening of the definition of reward to include the total value of employment is a relatively new concept. There is relatively little experience of total reward in the UK and precious little evidence of a widespread diffusion. Indeed, gauging the precise incidence of total reward rests largely on how one precisely defines it. The problem with the notion in its purest sense is that it includes many elements that are intangible, so quantifying its incidence is extraordinarily difficult. What's more, it is much more than simply a set of programmes: it's a process, an attitude to reward management, a mindset.

But amid this uncertainty, some reward analysts reckon that there is mounting evidence that total reward is becoming less of a minority pursuit. Duncan Brown, drawing on a large-scale survey of European organisations, is clear 'that this message is getting through to other organisations, and that a total reward approach is being adopted'.

A new wave approach?

This new-style approach to reward management reflects the latest metamorphism of the compensation and benefits profession. As the profession has continued to mature and a vast body of knowledge has developed, increasingly it has become evident that the battle to enlist the hearts and minds of all our employees involves much more than strategically-designed reward programmes. While few practitioners would now disagree with the proposition that it is essential for organisations to have a business-focused strategy, the most successful companies understand the importance of taking a much broader and holistic look at the factors involved in attraction, retention, development and motivation.

The Hay Group sees the evolution of the total reward concept as a reaction against established reward practice which implied everyone has a

price. These dominant reward approaches are now perceived as inadequate in a changing business environment. Helen Murlis and Steve Watson (2001) at the Hay Group argue that this new thinking represents a desire to break free of the perceived limitations of the past with its 'cost-based' approach and 'implicit work-life split' and concentrate on the talents and mindsets of employees.

As they explain:

It is a deal that enables fulfilment and engagement at work as well as at home. The focus is on what employers and their employees value and are prepared to contract on… It acknowledges 'emotional reward' – those aspects of reward that are compelling to the heart as well as the mind and reflect why people work and, given choice, why they select certain employers.

Total reward is not just another fad

The relentless chase for cheap and instant answers to intractable human resource problems has all too often been reflected in management 'fads' and 'fashions'. As organisations seek the magic cure in the battle to push them ahead of their rivals, they have been lured into adopting all manner of managerial and business practices which have, too often, been underdeveloped and inappropriate. Among the proliferation of dazzling new reward creations vying for the attention of the busy compensation specialist there are as many examples of failure as success.

It seems that the mythical search for the perfect pay system has become the HR expert's Holy Grail. So, is total reward just another quick fix based on little more than hot air and hype? Or is it likely to prove more durable than other fashionable business panaceas of recent years?

As with most HR innovations, there is nothing new in the total reward approach that has not been said before. The concept draws on various disciplines and is informed by some of the enduring tenets of motivation theory and the psychological contract:

◻ Few serious students of reward can have escaped the influence of the motivation theorists such as Maslow and Hertzberg, whose research underpins these ideas.

◻ Alfie Kohn, the American pay commentator, has long voiced the concerns of many theorists that financial incentives undermine intrinsic performance. Drawing on extensive psychological studies, Kohn warns that incentive plans, bonuses and other types of monetary reward, far from encouraging higher levels of achievement, disrupt employees' performance and motivation. This is because employees will think more about what they will earn than about the job itself.

◻ Jeffrey Pfeffer, Professor of Organisational Behaviour at Stanford Graduate School in the USA, has also consistently drawn our attention to the fact that while money can motivate, the stark reality is that cash alone cannot achieve higher levels of motivation and commitment among employees.

◻ Also across the Atlantic, the underlying theme of Huselid's work is that simultaneously combining several different HR and compensation techniques, as in the 'HR bundle', has more influence on performance than simply using individual practices. Similarly, a central thesis of the total reward supporters is that firms need to create a high level of 'internal consistency' or 'fit' among their HR and reward activities if they are to deliver superior organisational performance.

◻ The total reward literature also draws inspiration from the body of knowledge and research evidence on the psychological contract, which offers clues for organisations wishing to develop HR and reward policies that fulfil employees' changing priorities and beliefs.

So, there is certainly nothing really revolutionary in total reward. Indeed, the basic principles might seem like obvious common sense. Yet managers do not always follow them. That judgement is echoed by Murlis and Watson (2001):

Little of this is new and none of it is rocket science, but we sometimes have the opportunity to look at enduring truths in new ways, so, instead of dividing reward into an economic contract and a psychological contract, we can now break these down further to understand them better and, as compensation practitioners, to deliver them, as a whole, more effectively.

And Sandra O'Neal (1998) agrees:

Developing a total reward strategy is certainly not new. What does seem new, however, is the intensity with which organisations are pursuing such strategies.

But all too often organisations simply opt to throw money at people to prevent them from leaving and persist with inappropriate performance pay schemes. The real value of the total reward rhetoric lies in the revolution of perception it has wrought. These strategies are characterised by a much broader definition of what constitutes reward. Although these elements have always existed in the workplace, they have often been taken for granted and not actively managed. Under a total reward policy, all aspects of the work experience are recognised and prominence is given not only to remuneration but also to less tangible rewards.

The attraction of these total reward programmes lies in creating a reward melting pot that is suited to the organisation and makes it distinctive 'in ways that optimise employee satisfaction'. By daring to be different, by creating a unique employment offer that is more in tune with employees' needs and interests and more consistent with the expectations of a diverse workforce, these companies have been able to attract and retain talented people.

Is this 'people-centred' ethos likely to survive a downturn?

Could this hard-won emphasis on the human dimension of reward – with its underlying principle of people as one of the fundamental sources of value and competitive advantage – be undermined as companies trim costs with the onset of a harsher economic climate? Invariably in tough times the message that the financial aspects of reward are not in themselves sufficient to attract, retain and motivate people is easily overlooked by organisations eager to restructure and reinvent themselves. 'Regrettably, the transactional "economic model" all too often reasserts itself as soon as the chilly wind of recession makes itself felt. Underlying reward drivers are suppressed,' Murlis and Watson (2001) say.

So, is this new, sophisticated approach to reward management likely to survive if the hard times hit? Or is it all a luxury likely to be swept away in a period of adversity? Absolutely not, argue its admirers. This is surely the time when forward-thinking companies will decide it is imperative to assess their talent and their workplace environment to make sure that they are attracting – and keeping – the top performers needed to deliver long-term success. This approach is indeed 'recession resistant', according to the Hay Group (2002):

Engagement matters just as much in recession as it does in economic upturn. It is key to ensuring that organisations are as well placed as possible to benefit from an improving economic climate.

What's more, competition for talent is still ferocious, we are told, and will continue to be so despite the slowing world economy in the wake of the attacks on 11 September. Indeed, in the face of an economic downturn, the competition for talent between companies is likely to be even more hard fought.

A final word

It is a deal that enables fulfilment and engagement at work as well as home. The focus is on what employers and their employees value and are prepared to contract on. It is much closer to the model of motivation that psychologists would recognise.

Helen Murlis and Steve Watson (2001)

Table 1

Some consistent themes and components of total reward strategies have emerged. The notion of total reward as formulated in the various models is characterised by an approach which is:

- **Holistic** – it focuses on how organisations attract, retain and motivate employees to contribute to organisation success using an array of financial and non-financial rewards. It doesn't rely too heavily on pay and recognises that the reward package encompasses intrinsic aspects such as effective leadership, development, culture, recognition and work-life issues.

- **Best fit** – it adopts a contingency approach; total reward programmes need to be tailored to the organisation's own particular culture, structure, work processes and business objectives.

- **Integrative** – it delivers innovative rewards which are integrated with other human resource management policies and practices.

- **Strategic** – it aligns all aspects of reward to business strategy; total reward is driven by business needs and rewards the business activities, employee behaviour and values that support strategic goals and objectives

- **People-centred** – it recognises that people are a key source of sustainable competitive advantage and begins by focusing on what employees value in the total work environment.

- **Customised** – it identifies a flexible mix of rewards that offers choice and is better designed to meet employee needs, their lifestyle and stage of life.

- **Distinctive** – it uses a complex and diverse set of rewards to create a powerful and idiosyncratic employer brand that serves to differentiate the organisation from its rivals.

- **Evolutionary** – it is a long-term approach based on incremental rather than radical change.

Table 2

Hay's engaged performance model ™

The 'Engaged Performance Model' is the Hay Group's trademarked approach to total reward design. Hay Group (2002) defines engaged performance as:

A result that is achieved by stimulating employees' enthusiasm for their work and directing it toward organisational success. This result can only be achieved when employers offer an implicit contract to their employees that elicits specific positive behaviours aligned with the organisation's goals.

Its underlying theme is that people are central to business success. The business argument is that managers can elicit higher levels of 'discretionary effort' from people (and thereby deliver superior performance) by creating an engaged (enthusiastic and committed) workforce. As Hay puts it: 'The payoff is clear when organisations create the conditions for engagement and tap their employees' "discretionary effort": improved morale, higher productivity and a dramatic boost in financial performance.'

But attracting talent at all levels and gaining engagement and commitment to organisation success depends on more than pay systems. 'Pay levels may be the easiest aspects of reward with which rival businesses can compete against you, but they often fail to deliver sustained competitive advantage. Outstanding organisations have to be more subtle,' observes Hay. What is needed is a move to 'more holistic employment deals'.

The 'Engaged Performance Model' embraces not only tangible rewards – everything from competitive base salary and performance pay, to share schemes and benefits tailored to individual needs – but also the more 'intrinsic' aspects of reward – take, for example, freedom and autonomy, an acceptable work-life balance, and most crucially, an effective leadership and management style.

'Motivational drivers'

Hay's model (see Chapter 3) includes six elements which employees need before they direct their motivation towards their work.

◘ inspiration and values

◘ quality of work

◘ enabling environment

◘ tangible rewards

◘ work-life balance

◘ future growth/opportunity.

One of the six 'motivational drivers' is tangible reward. The first step is to get this right, argues Hay, because people who do not feel their remuneration is fair will be demotivated. But giving people competitive pay is necessary but not sufficient. 'Perhaps it's best to think of pay and benefits as merely a ticket to the game,' says the Hay Group. 'If you meet threshold levels for both, you get to play.

But you are not going to win unless you do a lot more.'

Employers must then turn their attention to meeting people's needs from other elements of 'engagement'. The Hay Group concludes: 'Using the engaged performance model to understand how better to tap employees' "discretionary effort", and get them as often as possible into real and sustained "flow", requires paying attention to all *six* drivers. It means understanding the needs and priorities of different segments of the employee population and taking clear, visible action to meet those needs.'

Inspirational leadership is the 'ultimate perk'

Hay reckons that 50 to 70 per cent of an organisation's climate – how it feels to work in particular environment, the atmosphere of a workplace – can be traced to leadership. Simply put, the leadership style of bosses strongly affects the organisational climate. In other words, good management creates a good climate, while poor management creates a poor climate. Both affect performance. This holds true in all sectors, says Hay.

At the heart of the engaged performance model is the idea that the quality of corporate leadership is a critical factor engaging employees for business success. So, for Hay, inspirational leadership is the ultimate motivator. 'In its absence, delivering on the other five elements of the engaged performance model is unlikely fully to engage employees.'

- Respected benefits consultants, such as Hay and Towers Perrin, are developing models of 'total reward' to help their clients get an 'edge' in the labour market.

- Although differing in detail and emphasis, their messages are broadly similar.

3 | Total reward models

Consultants and researchers have developed a plethora of total reward models. Here we examine the models formulated by four leading organisations: WorldatWork, Hay Group, Towers Perrin and Schuster-Zingheim and Associates.

WorldatWork

www.worldatwork.org

Background: Formerly the American Compensation Association, WorldatWork is one of the HR profession's oldest and most distinguished bodies. It is a not-for-profit association with a membership of more than 25,000 human resource professionals, consultants, educators and others, primarily in the United States and Canada.

Definition: Total rewards can be defined as all of the employer's available tools that may be used to attract, retain and motivate and satisfy employees.

Model

The WorldatWork model of total rewards has three main components:

1 *Compensation*

Made up of two basic elements: base pay and variable pay contingent upon performance or results achieved (for example, profit sharing, individual group/team incentives, equity-based compensation).

2 *Benefits*

'Benefits include various programmes designed to protect and ensure the employee's financial security and to reward the employee for time not worked.'

3 *The work experience*

These elements are the less tangible 'relational rewards that bind workers to the organisation more strongly because they satisfy an individual's intrinsic needs, such as personal development and fulfilment'.

There are five basic elements that should be addressed in the work experience component:

- *acknowledgement, appreciation and recognition* – including 'pat on the back', merchandise and time off

- *balance of work-life* – including flexible work schedules, conveniences services and childcare

- *culture* – including leadership, communication and organisational style

- *development* – including learning

opportunities, coaching and employee involvement

- *environment* – including job content, autonomy, public perception of company.

Factors influencing the reward mix

Overlaying the total reward model are two key factors:

Figure 1 | WorldatWork 'The Professional Association for Compensation Benefits and Total Rewards'

◘ *internal influences* – which include your organisation's core ideology, funds available, internal organisational culture and its desired behaviours, business strategies and competitive environment – in essence what makes your organisation tick

◘ *external influences* – which include the economy, general business environment, government mandates, labour pool and other forces beyond your organisation's control.

A final word

Studies show that organisations that offer a compelling future, individual growth, a positive workplace and total rewards approach – balanced to match their business strategies – are most likely to attract and retain the best and brightest talent. And they are most likely to win in the marketplace.

WorldatWork Web link

www.worldatwork.org/feature/tr.html

Hay Group

www.haygroup.com

Background: The Hay Group is one of the world's leading independent management consultancies, with 73 offices in 35 countries. For more than 50 years it has 'helped organisations around the globe achieve their goals by addressing critical people issues'.

Definition: 'Engaged performance is the way Hay looks at reward design. It is not just about pay systems – reward is more than just remuneration. Engaged performance is about understanding why working for a particular organisation is attractive to different kinds of individuals. It considers the financial, motivational and practical aspects of work. Engaged performance looks at the "heart and mind" reasons why people work; and why they work for you. The business premise is that the best organisations have "engaged, performing people that achieve business results".'

Model

Hay's model (Figure 2, page 22) is made up of six elements:

1 Inspiration/values

◘ reputation of organisation

◘ organisational values and behaviours

◘ quality of leadership

◘ risk sharing

◘ recognition

◘ communication.

2 Quality of work

▫ perception of the value of work

▫ challenge/interest

▫ opportunities for achievement

▫ freedom and autonomy

▫ workload

▫ quality of work relationship.

3 Enabling environment

▫ physical environment

▫ tools and equipment

▫ job training (current position)

▫ information and processes

▫ safety/personal security.

Figure 2

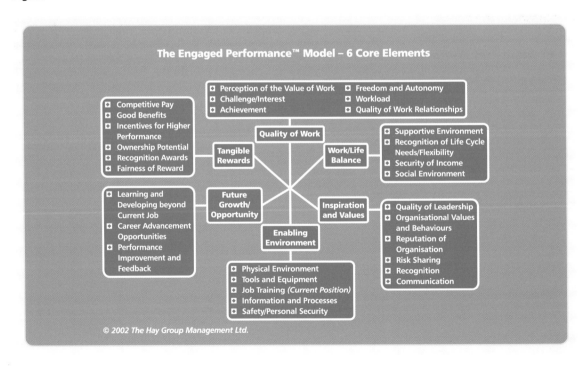

The Engaged Performance™ Model – 6 Core Elements

▫ Perception of the Value of Work   ▫ Freedom and Autonomy
▫ Challenge/Interest   ▫ Workload
▫ Achievement   ▫ Quality of Work Relationships

Quality of Work

▫ Competitive Pay
▫ Good Benefits
▫ Incentives for Higher Performance
▫ Ownership Potential
▫ Recognition Awards
▫ Fairness of Reward

Tangible Rewards

Work/Life Balance

▫ Supportive Environment
▫ Recognition of Life Cycle Needs/Flexibility
▫ Security of Income
▫ Social Environment

▫ Learning and Developing beyond Current Job
▫ Career Advancement Opportunities
▫ Performance Improvement and Feedback

Future Growth/ Opportunity

Inspiration and Values

▫ Quality of Leadership
▫ Organisational Values and Behaviours
▫ Reputation of Organisation
▫ Risk Sharing
▫ Recognition
▫ Communication

Enabling Environment

▫ Physical Environment
▫ Tools and Equipment
▫ Job Training (*Current Position*)
▫ Information and Processes
▫ Safety/Personal Security

© 2002 The Hay Group Management Ltd.

4 *Tangible rewards*

- competitive pay
- good benefits
- incentives for higher performance
- ownership potential
- recognition awards
- fairness of reward.

5 *Work-life balance*

- supportive environment
- recognition of life cycle needs/flexibility
- security of income
- social support.

6 *Future growth/opportunity*

- learning and developing beyond current job
- career advancement opportunities
- performance improvement and feedback.

A final word

Pay levels may be the easiest aspects of reward with which rival businesses can compete against you, but they often fail to deliver sustained competitive advantage. Outstanding organisations have to be more subtle. Other, more intrinsic aspects of reward are much harder to replicate and sustain and are the source of longer-term competitive advantage. These usually vary according to the generation, culture and economic standing of prospective employees. Building your offer around their specific needs will lead to success in attraction, retention and motivation.

> *'Companies can either balance the four components or emphasise one over the others, but they must provide a total reward package that attracts the type of talent they need and want.'*

Hay Group Web link

www.haygroup.co.uk/Transform_your_business/
Products_and_Services/HR_Consulting/
Reward_Management.asp

Towers Perrin

www.towers.com

Background: Towers Perrin is one of the world's largest independent management consulting firms and has 'provided innovative advice and assistance to large organisations in both the private and public sectors for more than 60 years'. It has over 9,000 employees and 78 offices in 23 countries.

Definition: 'Total rewards embraces the investments you make in your people and the things your employees value in their work. By managing rewards in an integrated, holistic way, you can successfully align employee behaviours and rewards with a company's business objectives, for the ultimate benefit of employer, employee and shareholder alike… Ultimately, through our total rewards approach, you can achieve two fundamental objectives: manage and optimise your investments in people; and engage the workforce in delivering superior levels of performance.'

Figure 3

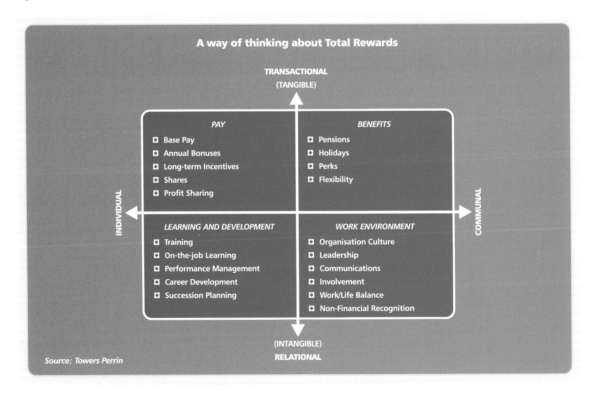

Model

Towers Perrin uses a simple matrix to help consider the total rewards strategy in an organisation. It is made up of four quadrants which 'embrace the full range of things that employees value in their work, so there's a compelling proposition for people to join and stay with your company'.

◘ The upper two quadrants – pay and benefits – represent *transactional rewards*. These are financial in nature, and are essential to recruit and retain staff, but can be easily copied by competitors.

◘ By contrast, *relational rewards* – the sort produced by the lower two quadrants of learning and development and work environment – are essential to enhancing the value of the upper quadrants.

The real power comes when an organisation combines relational and transactional awards. Says Towers Perrin:

The combination of transactional and relational rewards creates broad, flexible exchanges that lead to employee commitment to common goals, values, and long-term objectives.

A final word

It is only when all of the elements of reward strategies (or total reward) are considered holistically, and in line with business and human resource strategies, that the total spend on employees can deliver most value to the business. Given the range of things people value – and recognising the impact of age, culture and other factors – the key is determining which rewards will produce the greatest impact on the employees that the company has identified as most important to success. The companies who are going to succeed not only will have to offer competitive total rewards, they will have to find ways to allow employees to individualise and personalise those total reward packages.

Towers Perrin Web link

www.towers.com/towers/locations/uk/
totalrewards.htm

Schuster-Zingheim and Associates
www.paypeopleright.com

Background: Schuster-Zingheim and Associates is a pay consulting firm based in Los Angeles, founded in 1995 by Jay R. Schuster and Patricia K. Zingheim. As leading exponents of the 'new pay' philosophy, Schuster and Zingheim struck a chord with many reward specialists because they provided a convincing vision of how reward systems should operate in the future, with a particular emphasis on strategic reward and variable pay.

Definition: 'Total rewards integrate total pay with a compelling future, individual growth and a positive workplace to create a win-win partnership between the company and its workforce that enhances effectiveness and advances overall business objectives'.

Figure 4

Model

Schuster and Zingheim view total rewards in any company as having four 'interlocked and directly related components'.

Schuster and Zingheim's four 'interlocked and directly related' components	
Individual growth	**Total pay**
◘ Investment in people	◘ Base pay
◘ Development and training	◘ Variable pay (cash and stock)
◘ Performance management	◘ Benefits or indirect pay
◘ Career enhancement	◘ Recognition and celebration
Compelling future	**Positive workplace**
◘ Vision and values	◘ People focus
◘ Company growth and success	◘ Leadership
◘ Company image and reputation	◘ Colleagues
◘ Stakeholdership	◘ Work itself
◘ Win-win over time	◘ Involvement
	◘ Trust and commitment
	◘ Open communications

Schuster and Zingheim (2002)

A final word

When more jobs are chasing fewer people, companies must provide a better workforce deal that involves the four total reward components outlined below. Companies can either balance the four components or emphasise one over the others, but they must provide a total reward package that attracts the type of talent they need and want. For example, some companies may be weak in positive workplace but have very strong total pay to make up for the difficult work environment. Other companies may have weaker total pay but develop people, provide a positive workplace, and have a compelling future that people want to support and be a part of Schuster-Zingheim.

- It is becoming recognised that the pious mantra 'our people are our greatest asset', which has for so long adorned company 'mission statements' and annual reports, is actually true.

- The ever-increasing difficulty of recruiting and retaining good people means that the needs and wants of such people will have to be met by employers.

4 | Employees are critical to business success

In our new knowledge- and service-based economy, in which key skill shortages are increasingly apparent, people costs not only typically represent a much higher proportion of total expenditure, but those people really are your organisation's most important asset. If you do not reward them in the most effective way, ensuring that you recognise and reinforce what will make the business a success, and changing the former as the latter shifts, then you are increasingly likely to be put out of business by someone else who does.

Duncan Brown (2001)

Employers are finally waking up to the colossal costs of their most able employees' deserting the company. There is now a genuine belief that people are the primary sustainable source of competitive advantage in the modern economy. For better or worse, it is people – their intellects, creativity, skills, commitment and leadership – who shape companies in an ever-changing business environment.

So, a central strategic issue for organisations is how to recruit and retain employees' knowledge-based skills, their intellectual capital and then gain commitment to organisational success. Or, as the Hay Group (2002) puts it:

If people are a key source of competitive advantage, their engagement and performance levels can make or break any organisation's strategy. Ultimately, delivering strategy is about hiring the right people and motivating them to deliver results.

The importance of people to business strategy and success

It is possible to discern a number of key trends that have intensified the need for employers to think creatively about what they are going to do to stop their people walking out of the door. And they are rewriting the rules of reward management.

Employees are now the most critical resource for any organisation

Pivotal to the emergence of total reward has been the rise of the 'human capital movement'. The crux of this idea is that 'building and leveraging' human capital is the source of sustained competitive advantage. Much contemporary thinking in business strategy emphasises that employees – rather than finance or technology – really are vitally important to organisational success in developed economies.

Most companies talk a pretty good story about the value of their employees, but the harsh truth for all too many is that their actions do not back up their best intentions. Organisations can no longer afford to view their employees simply as interchangeable parts. The more switched-on businesses have realised that their best people matter – even more so when it is such a ghastly struggle to find enough key talent to fill the available jobs.

'If you consider your employees' needs as well as your business needs, you may very well have an easier time satisfying both.'

Knowledge workers are becoming a key source of competitive advantage

Information technology has revolutionised many organisations – and quickly – producing a growing demand for new skills and knowledge and creating greater flexibility in how, when, where and with whom work is accomplished. Many organisations would now endorse the view that they operate in a vastly different employment environment, in which knowledge workers are central to organisational success. In today's business community, intellectual capital is at a premium and technology is transforming the way we do business.

Labour turnover costs are escalating

Today's tight labour market has had at least one salutary effect: managers are becoming ever more aware of the cost of their most prized employees' jumping ship.

All told, the latest labour turnover survey by the Chartered Institute of Personnel and Development estimates that replacing a managerial or professional employee is likely to cost on average £6,000. The 629-company survey discovered that no fewer than one in four employees left his/her organisation in 2000, the highest figure since the survey began in 1995.

A second large-scale research project, by the Hay Group (2001), covering 1 million employees at more than 330 companies worldwide, revealed that about one-third of employees plan to resign within two years. According to its calculations, each manager or professional who departs costs the company the equivalent of 18 months' salary. The cost of replacing an hourly-paid worker is roughly 0.5 times his/her annual salary.

The workforce is becoming more diverse

As the next chapter illustrates, demographic and social changes have had a profound impact on the profile of the UK's workforce, with a corresponding change in social values.

Total reward may offer a solution to your recruitment and retention difficulties

Organisations are perpetually under pressure to create an employment relationship that will help them nurture, manage and extract maximum value from a key corporate asset – their employees. The employment relationship and how it is managed have become fundamental to organisational success. Indeed, the big question facing many organisations is this: how can we engage the hearts and minds of all our employees?

Because turnover costs are so high and people are so important to the modern business, companies need to take serious measures to improve recruitment and retention. People leave jobs for all sorts of reasons, but a recurring finding in much of the research is that dissatisfaction with pay is rarely a prime motivation for moving on. It's possible to overlook the obvious fact that people are unlikely to stay in a work environment that is stifling and out of touch with employee needs.

The key theme running throughout the Hay Group's 2001 study is that employees are most likely to leave when their skills and talents are not properly developed or when superiors fail to take an interest in their career development. Above all, employees are much more likely to walk out of the door at the end of the day and not return when they perceive a lack of clear direction on the part of managers.

Yet the traditional solution to recruitment and retention difficulties is to 'put more money on the table'. But as this tactic is used by all too many organisations, it does not afford competitive advantage and immediately raises costs.

Leading organisations, it seems, will need to primp and preen themselves like Hollywood divas in a bid to seduce the top talent. Rather than simply offering more enticing pay packages to give them the edge in luring and keeping these valued employees who are so critical to high-quality work and customer service, they will need to think about reward in a much broader sense, including the work environment. And training and development is, of course, a much-overlooked cornerstone of an effective recruitment and retention policy.

As Duncan Brown (2001) remarks:

Without a much stronger emphasis on meeting employee needs and having the reward processes in place to do that, the potential returns of a more strategic approach to reward management will not be realised.

> **'...each manager or professional who departs costs the company the equivalent of 18 months' salary.'**

So it is perhaps unsurprising that a growing number of organisations have come to embrace the notion of more cohesive total reward strategies. More organisations are taking this concept seriously as they have come to realise that tailoring the total reward package to meet individual needs may be the most effective way of responding to recruitment and retention difficulties.

If you consider your employees' needs as well as your business needs, you may very well have an easier time satisfying both.

A final word

Organisations are recognising that people are the key engines that drive success. Attracting the best people to your organisation is becoming increasingly difficult as their expectations and aspirations rise. In the 'war for talent' you need to provide a rewarding environment which attracts the people you need and provides an environment in which they can flourish.

Hay Group

- **Today's workforce is much more demanding in its need for work-life balance. Employers who do not respond to this risk losing their staff to others who do.**
- **Different generations within the workforce have different needs – a one-size-fits-all approach to reward is no longer appropriate.**

5 | A changing employment landscape

It is simply no longer possible to create a set of rewards that is universally appealing to all employees or to address a series of complex business issues through a single set of solutions.

Sandra O'Neal (1998)

Demographic shifts and changes in the very structure of society have had a significant impact on the profile of the UK's workforce. Today's workforce is becoming ever more mobile and more diverse.

- Their differences include not only ethnicity and gender, but also values and expectations.

- Changes in family and social values have seen more women, working parents, dual-income households and single parents enter the market.

- More and more people have caring responsibilities – not just for their children but, as the workforce ages, for elderly relatives too.

- Today's workforce includes several distinct generations – each, so it is suggested, with a different perspective of the employee/employer relationship.

There is also increasing evidence that employees have now come to view their work differently, a trend that is said to have given rise to an overall shift in workplace values. They want greater control of what they are doing, ideally undertaking more meaningful work. They seek balanced lives.

> **'Valuing each employee includes understanding that not everyone wants to work the same way or be rewarded the same way.'**

Young people, in particular, are supposed to be looking for different things, often beyond monetary rewards, from their working lives today and employers are having to respond. A clutch of studies indicates that younger employees place a far higher priority on the work environment and learning and development than on traditional elements of reward (Tulgan, 2000; Watson Wyatt 2002).

As a study by the Hay Group puts it:

New generations of employees joining the labour market in developed economies are now demanding different things from employers and the workplace.

According to the authors of this report, Helen Murlis and Steve Watson (2001), these new entrants to the labour market are 'more knowledgeable, reward conscious and also often more cynical about employer behaviour'. What's more, they are accustomed to being treated as clients/customers and are less tolerant of below-par performance.

The inescapable conclusion, according to Murlis and Watson, is that it is time for a reappraisal of reward management:

The old recipes for the reward package do not seem to work in the same way any more. Employment is less and less seen as a cold effort/ reward transaction.

The challenge for reward professionals

So the assumption is that job-related attitudes, expectations and priorities are changing. Today's employees want to know what employers are going to do to enhance their work experience and help balance their work and personal lives. In truth, what employees want is not entirely novel, but what they are willing to give up to contract to achieve their goal is intensifying. Understanding these changes and responding to them is a commercial necessity. As Sandra O'Neal (1998) explains:

Today's workers are clear about these employment changes, and they are prepared to contribute, but at a price. Increasingly, that price is not merely pay and benefits but relational rewards of learning and development and work environment.

One of the main priorities for the HR function in the current climate is straightforward: to do as much as possible to attract people to your organisation, win their commitment and engagement to work, and then stop the very best talent walking out of the door.

According to the main exponents of total reward, the changes will have a profound impact on reward management. Simply stated, human resource and reward professionals must rethink their directions and realign their focus. And the long-term picture of a declining birth rate and ageing population should focus the minds of companies even more strongly.

The cardinal rules of reward need to be rewritten. For Duncan Brown (2001) the 'alignment of your reward practices with employee values and needs is every bit as important as alignment with business goals, and critical to the realisation of the latter.' The research evidence on motivation at work and the psychological contract tells us that individual characteristics help shape the different values employees place on pay, benefits, and the various elements of the 'work experience'. These values may vary according to the age, gender, culture and economic standing of employees.

WorldatWork (2000), the US reward association, has a strong message for pay decision-makers: rather than imposing a standardised programme, the values and expectations of an increasingly diverse workforce must be met flexibly with choice in the reward programme, which must be responsive to individual needs. 'The challenge is to develop and implement a flexible programme that capitalises on this diverse workforce. Valuing each employee includes understanding that not everyone wants to work the same way or be rewarded the same way. To achieve excellence, companies need a portfolio of total reward plans,' WorldatWork says.

Offering the right mix of rewards is vital, it seems, if you want to influence behaviour in critical employee groups.

Work-life policies rising up the reward agenda

The trend towards an ever-ageing population, a high proportion of women in full-time employment and a dramatic increase in lone parents and carers for elderly people has meant that more people have caring responsibilities and a pressing imperative to balance those responsibilities outside the workplace with their working lives. Additionally, there is an increased desire among fathers to become involved in the nurturing of children.

As the workforce has become diverse, with an array of lifestyles and family structures, the need for companies to adopt arrangements to accommodate the requirements arising from their employee's family responsibilities has intensified.

Today's employees are also bringing a new set of values to their careers. Workers are willing to sacrifice more money today than they once were in order to achieve a greater work-life balance.

A whole catalogue of studies suggest that employers worldwide are recognising of their own accord that there is a significant business case to provide opportunities to help their workforce balance their work lives with the rest of their lives – with a pay-back of enhanced commitment, better effectiveness and productivity, and improved recruitment and retention. More and more companies are allowing employees to determine when they work, where they work and how they work. A wide range of work-life options such as compressed working hours, flexible work schedules and family leave – and flexible benefit packages to support them – are now all the rage. When a company helps its employees balance their work lives with the rest of their lives, they feel a stronger commitment to the organisation.

Work-life policies must be strategically managed

But there is clearly a danger that all too often these programmes, policies and benefits are viewed as little more than a piecemeal collection of single-issue HR benefits. Total reward recognises that employees want, and in many instances demand, the ability to balance their lifestyle and their work. But it ensures that work-life initiatives are part of a well-integrated reward and HR strategy.

There is no question that that work-life policies will count for little unless they are rooted in business strategies and employees feel fully involved in the redesign of work practices. That is the powerful message from a three-year study by the influential Work in America Institute. *Holding a Job, Having a Life: Strategies for Change* illustrates that when companies adopt a strategic, systematic approach to addressing work-life issues as part of broader changes in work processes and cultures, they are more likely to report 'significant business gains' – including better retention, higher productivity and reduced absenteeism.

'The cardinal rules of reward need to be rewritten.'

As the Institute explains:

The work-life redesigns described in the report differ from management-driven, top-down re-engineering, because they encourage strong employee involvement and encompass both work-life needs and strategic business objectives. Addressing both dimensions creates a synergy that improves employees' lives and unleashes individual and team creativity.

A final word

A critical principle is that the returns offered by the employer are the primary determinants of the contributions provided by employees. That is, what employees are willing to give to the organisation is determined in large part by what the employer is willing to give to the employee.

Milkovich and Bloom (1998)

- The 'psychological contract' requires that organisations are seen as 'caring employers'.

- Work is no longer regarded as just a means of paying the bills – it must also offer meaningful occupation, and even be 'fun'.

- Reward structures must be flexible enough to accommodate a wide range of reward expectations of employees.

6 | The importance of non-financial rewards

The key to meeting both business and employee needs successfully is the definition and delivery of a positive psychological contract, defining the mutual obligations, contributions and rewards for each party. This can also serve as an effective brand and differentiator in the recruitment market, which is much more difficult for competitors to replicate than individual pay practices.

Duncan Brown (2001)

We have been told time and time again that cash is not all that matters. The extensive research on pay and motivation and a crop of texts on the psychological contract suggests that many factors beyond the purely monetary motivate and engage people at work. What is clear is that simplistic assumptions about the power of money to motivate have led many organisations to develop simplistic performance-related pay schemes or other forms of incentives.

In fact, we know only too well that employees place a great deal of emphasis on intangible rewards when deciding where to work and the level of commitment to give their work.

Many managers may see performance-based rewards as the route to commercial success, but the research on employee perception confirms that managers need to address the whole of the psychological contract. Policies that focus on managing only the financial elements of the psychological contract will not be sufficient to stimulate higher levels of commitment to the organisation and higher levels of motivation to produce optimal results.

> *'...total reward processes can help you clarify the psychological contract and contribute to the development of a more productive and mutually supporting relationship.'*

What come across loud and clear from this research is that to build employee commitment to the business and engage the workforce in delivering superior levels of performance requires that organisations manage all their investments in people. By thoroughly assessing and then addressing what it is that employees need in the package to feel well rewarded and motivated, you can start to create a working environment that will help you to hold on to and inspire your best people.

Looking ahead, the focus will be on a much broader, more balanced and customised array of rewards. Many organisations – especially traditional ones – will need to rethink their entire approach to recruiting, retaining and rewards design.

Money is not the only motivator

After hearing it from so many voices, more organisations need to acknowledge that pay is not the only, nor often the ultimate, motivator at work. This is not to say that pay is unimportant to people. It is vital to get it right – otherwise, much damage can be done. If individuals are not treated fairly, pay becomes a symbol of the unfairness and a source of dissatisfaction.

And clearly, some employees are more motivated by money than others. All you can be certain about is that a multitude of interdependent factors is involved in motivating employees. Money is only one of those factors, which may work for some personality types in some circumstances, but may not prove effective for other people in different circumstances.

So the significance of pay as a means of attracting, retaining and providing tangible rewards for people is not to be underestimated. But as a means of generating long-term commitment and motivation, pay has to be viewed as only part of the solution. It is the non-financial rewards that will ultimately make the difference. But as Brown (2001) sees it:

These non-financial items are often ignored and are therefore hugely under-leveraged in many organisations.

Organisations need to 'de-emphasise pay'

Jeffrey Pfeffer (1998a and 1998b), Professor of Organisational Behaviour at the Stanford Graduate School in the USA, and one of the world's leading authorities on human resource and compensation practice, has published a devastating demolition job on managers' reliance on expensive fictions about how to reward people and why. He observes that there is a tendency for organisations to overemphasise pay as a solution to all of their performance or management problems. Says Pfeffer (1998b):

Leaders must come to see pay for what it is: just one element in a set of management practices that can either build or reduce commitment, teamwork, and performance.

His central thesis is that pay is no substitute for a working environment 'high on trust, fun and meaningful work'. He has a harsh warning for managers who ignore that message: they will be doomed to continual tinkering with pay which, at the end of the day, will accomplish very little – at great cost:

People do work for money – but they work even more for meaning in their lives. In fact, they work to have fun. Companies that ignore this fact are essentially bribing their employees and will pay the price in a lack of loyalty and commitment.

By portraying pay as the ultimate reward, organisations are telling their employees that money is basically all they provide for those who work for them. 'Managers can fight the myth that people are primarily motivated by money by de-emphasising pay and not portraying it as the main thing you get from working in a particular company,' says Pfeffer (1998b). 'Emphasising pay as the primary reward encourages people to come and stay for the wrong reasons.' The result? Intrinsic motivation is undermined. 'Most perniciously, in their emphasis on financial incentives,' writes Pfeffer (1998a), 'managers and their organisations neglect and ignore other, non-financial aspects of the motivation environment' (Pfeffer 1998a).

Relational rewards 'bind' employees to the organisation

The influential US writers Milkovich and Bloom (1998), too, lay bare the myth that financial rewards are all that matters when it comes to 'binding' the employee to the organisation. Their work's merit is in reminding readers that many factors beyond the purely monetary encourage the sort of behaviours that distinguish outstanding from ordinary performance, and which create the 'mindset' required for your staff to go that extra mile.

Financial returns alone cannot extract the unique, value-adding ideas and behaviour possessed by employees. Financial returns alone are ineffective in creating the common mindset that creates people's willingness to share the insights and tacit knowledge required to achieve and sustain advantage.

What really attracts, motivates and engages workers, according to Milkovich and Bloom, is a much broader and balanced mix of 'transactional' rewards (the tangible, financial elements such as pay, benefits and hours) coupled with 'relational' rewards (the intangible non-pay and benefits elements that run the whole gamut from the work environment to cultural issues, employee involvement to development opportunities).

They are clear that it is these relational rewards that address the unique individual needs of employees.

Relational returns may bind individuals more strongly to the organisation because they can answer those special individual needs that cannot be met as effectively with economic returns.

The received wisdom is that while the transactional forms – the pay and benefit elements of total compensation – can have an immediate and powerful effect, it will not necessarily last long. There is little doubt that focusing solely on these financial rewards creates instrumental relationships that can be easily matched by rivals. All of which leads to the inescapable conclusion that it is much more difficult for rivals to replicate the more intrinsic aspects of reward. The idea is that relational rewards allow the organisation the opportunity to differentiate itself from rivals and create competitive advantage.

Organisations must manage the entire psychological contract

By now most of you will be familiar with the notion of the psychological contract. It is a concept that has attracted a great deal of attention in recent years. Although there is no single definition of the psychological contract, in essence it refers to the mix of mutual assumptions, expectations, promises and obligations that exist between individual employees and employers.

In short, this concept expresses the combination of beliefs held by an individual and the employer about what they expect of one another. But why exactly is it so important? Put simply, the state of the contract can greatly influence employee behaviour and attitudes. A positive psychological contract is predicted to lead to higher employee satisfaction, higher levels of motivation and higher levels of commitment to the organisation. There is an assumption that any 'shortfall' between employees' expectations and what the employer delivers is associated with lower satisfaction with work, and results in a higher propensity to leave the organisation.

Professor David Guest of King's College, London, who is one of the leading UK writers on the subject, and his colleagues at Birkbeck College, argue that the state of the psychological contract is defined by:

- employees' general perceptions of 'fairness of treatment' at work

- trust in their management and, in particular, trust that the organisation keeps to its promises or commitments

- delivery of the 'deal' with respect to key promises and obligations.

The psychological contract tells us something very important about what employees actually want from the employment relationship. It enumerates what employees feel the organisation owes them in terms of an array of issues – pay, training, career development, personal growth, respect, autonomy, responsibility, leadership, employee involvement, interesting work and job security – and what they receive in practice. As a new report succinctly puts it:

It has gained prominence because it holds out the promise of a framework that can help us understand the impact of changes in the work environment on the employment relationship. (Thompson and Heron 2001).

Importantly, the psychological contract highlights that there are other areas beyond the purely monetary that organisations need to address in order to foster a positive shift in employee behaviour and encourage employees to voluntarily commit to fully contribute to the competitive success of the organisation. The 'deal' is not just about offering employees more money. It requires focusing on more than pay. It requires, we are told, focusing on total rewards. Managers must address the whole of the psychological contract: everything from good job design to employee involvement. It is these relational dimensions of the employment relationship that are seen as crucial in determining trust, motivation, work performance and job satisfaction.

But if these different aspirations are to be met, they first need to be identified and understood. So, at the outset it is vital that companies discover what those employees within your business who can make a difference really value, and then you must be willing to take the risks necessary to include these reward elements in the overall package.

The reward system is central to the psychological contract – it is the most visible aspect of the employment 'deal'. As Duncan Brown (2001) writes:

Pay and formal reward and employment practices are one of the most tangible symbols of a company's culture and employment offering, inextricably intertwined with them. Therefore they are critical to demonstrating that the employer is delivering on its side of the employment bargain.

Well managed, the reward system can act as a powerful vehicle for stimulating or reinforcing the process of organisational or cultural change. Badly managed, it can become a source of dissatisfaction undermining the deal.

So organisations need to review their reward systems in order to ensure that they consistently reinforce a positive psychological contract. It may be that total reward processes can help you clarify the psychological contract and contribute to the development of a more productive and mutually supporting relationship.

Organisations that can strike the right balance between extrinsic and intrinsic reward will reinforce the employment deal and make it more real for employees:

◻ by providing financial rewards through schemes that reward the business activities, behaviour and values that support strategic goals and objectives

◻ by offering non-financial rewards that address each employee's needs.

'...cash is not all that matters.'

According to this view, by gaining a thorough understanding of what employees expect from the employer in return for their contribution, organisations can identify how their reward practices can help to deliver the required deal. Companies must begin thinking about reward more broadly. Mixing and matching rewards within a broader reward framework aligned with business needs, companies can reallocate their investment to match what employees say they most value, ensure organisation success and communicate the integrated package versus a kaleidoscope of individual components.

A final word

The total value of employment, comprising both relational and financial returns, creates broad, flexible exchanges of deals with employees. Multiple deals encompass a broad range of exchanges and can help create commitment to common values, goals and the pursuit of mutually beneficial long-term objectives.

Milkovich and Bloom (1998)

- There is evidence that increasing numbers of employers are coming to realise the value of offering 'bundles' of benefits.

- Four elements of a total rewards approach have been identified: pay, benefits, environment and development.

7 | Why we need an integrated approach to reward

Human resources personnel used to be able to solve their problems via single-silo solutions to pay, benefits, training or labour… Bundling human resources disciplines to address these complexities results in what is called 'total rewards'.

Sandra O'Neal (1998)

Few of us interested and involved in reward can have escaped the avalanche of books, articles and research studies extolling the virtues of aligning reward management to the strategic agenda of the organisation. Employers are urged to move from relatively passive, reactive compensation and benefit programmes of the past, and embrace reward strategies that support the pursuit of broader organisational objectives and development. Greater integration between pay and business strategy is the secret of success.

And there is some empirical evidence that more and more UK organisations have indeed decided that a strategically-designed reward management perspective could give them the edge in a rapidly-changing business environment.

The overriding theme running throughout the reward strategy literature, and indeed practice, is on the desirability of organisations adopting 'vertical alignment' of reward programmes with business goals. Today's reward decisions are intended to be aligned with the business strategy and signal valued employee behaviour. But Duncan Brown (2001), one of the UK's most influential reward strategy thinkers, urges practitioners to remember that reward needs to fit not only strategic business objectives but also be consistent with other HR initiatives:

Far too little account has been taken of the need for horizontal alignment between all of the various reward and HR programmes.

All too often the bewildering array of programmes in the employment offer are disconnected from one another and from broader business strategy. Rather than developing an integrated and mutually supporting range of processes, problems are commonly dealt with in an *ad hoc*, unstructured and piecemeal fashion. In some cases, they have sent conflicting messages to employees, which weaken the overall power of your reward strategy.

Brown is surely not alone in thinking that adopting a more integrated approach to all reward practices with each other, and with other HR programmes, *will be much more effective for your organisation in the longer term than single 'one-hit' interventions.*

The notion of HR 'bundles'

Recognising this requirement for greater 'horizontal alignment' fits in neatly with contemporary thinking in human resource management. Research is now emerging that focuses on the notion of HR 'systems'. According to this view, organisations need to create a high level of 'internal consistency' or 'fit' among their HR initiatives if they are to deliver superior organisational performance.

'Greater integration between pay and business strategy is the secret of success.'

Its underlying theme is that simultaneously combining several different HR and compensation techniques in coherent 'bundles' of practices has a much more powerful and longer-lasting influence on performance than single interventions.

As the UK academics Annette Cox and John Purcell (1998) note:

The existence of relatively sophisticated human resource practices internally coherent one with the other, as in the 'HR bundle', seems to be critical to the successful implementation of any pay system change, and employee involvement practices seem also to be a prerequisite. This suggests that the

real source of benefit in reward strategies lies in complex linkages with other human resource management policies and practices.

They add:

Achieving the right architecture of the HR bundle, its particular idiosyncratic configuration in each organisation, may be more important than the individual brick of any single policy or practice.

A final word

A total rewards framework is also an important means of strategically integrating and relating the range of reward schemes in an organisation. Developing and integrating a 'bundle' of rewards programmes that apply across all four quadrants of a total rewards approach – pay, benefits, environment and development – helps to maximise the motivational impact of your reward strategy.

Duncan Brown (2001)

- A total reward strategy can bring benefits to the employer in three areas: enhanced business performance; better recruitment and retention of staff; and a more motivated workforce.

- In essence, it comes down to the employer being regarded as an 'employer of choice'.

8 | What are the attractions of total reward strategies?

Through total rewards, companies are able to mold, blend and shape a unique rewards package that appeals specifically to the type of employees they want to attract and retain.

WorldatWork (2000)

The hype about total reward is strong – but will it deliver? Yes, is the only conclusion to be drawn from a catalogue of studies extolling the virtues of this concept. Its supporters argue that organisations that offer a compelling future, individual growth, a positive workplace in the context of a total reward approach – balanced to match their business strategies – are most likely to attract and retain the best and brightest talent. Employees enjoy higher levels of job satisfaction, while employers enjoy increased levels of motivation and performance. The argument is that this approach can have a positive and lasting impact on the bottom line.

According to one of its strongest proponents, companies that consciously take a holistic approach to total rewards have a 'proprietary advantage' over their business rivals.

With the right total reward strategy and programmes in place, the organisation can reasonably expect three interrelated outcomes:

◻ improved business results

◻ enhanced recruitment and retention

◻ a positive shift in employee behaviour and contributions.

What, then, do organisations hope to achieve by embracing total reward strategies? From the business viewpoint it is possible to discern six main attractions of moving to a total rewards approach (see Table 4).

Improved recruitment and retention

Perhaps the principal business case for offering your employees all-embracing total reward packages is that this approach gives you the edge in the attraction and retention battle, along with improved performance.

There was a time when pay rises and promotions were the most commonplace retention tools. But keeping your most valued employees requires a lot more than quick fixes and piecemeal approaches such as 'golden handcuffs' and loyalty bonuses. It requires a much broader array of tools on the part of employers. 'They soon learn that throwing money at recruitment and retention is subject to the law of diminishing returns,' Helen Murlis and Steve Watson (2001) say.

Cash is a weak tactic in the overall reward strategy: it is too easily replicated. Intrinsic reward is far more difficult to emulate.

Numerous studies show that employees look at the overall employment package when deciding whether to stay with or join an organisation (Hay Group, 2001; Incomes Data Services, 2000). As highly desirable job candidates explore their options with various companies, supporters argue that those with total rewards have a competitive advantage because they are able to show the 'total value' of their employment package.

Progressive-thinking companies try to create a working environment that not only brings out the best in top performers, but also attracts, nurtures and retains the brightest talent. They understand the importance of engaging all their people.

By focusing on monetary rewards it is all too easy to overlook ways of succeeding that competitors cannot readily copy. As Pfeffer has reminded us, what really gives an employer the edge as he/she struggles to woo and retain scarce talent is appealing to the beliefs, personal values and lifestyle choices of today's employees. 'Any organisation believing it can solve its attraction, retention, and motivation problems solely by its

compensation system is probably not spending as much time and effort as it should on the work environment – on defining its jobs, on creating its culture, and on making work fun and meaningful,' says Pfeffer (1998b).

It is a question of time and attention of scarce managerial resources. The time and attention spent managing the reward system are not available to devote to other aspects of the work environment that in the end may be much more critical to success.

So it seems that companies that consciously take a holistic approach to total reward may then be able to push themselves ahead of rivals in the recruitment and retention race. For Sandra O'Neal (1998), a total reward strategy is critical to addressing the issues created by recruitment and retention.

It can help create a work experience that meets the needs of employees and encourages them to contribute extra effort, by developing a deal that addresses a broad range of issues and by spending reward dollars where they will be most effective in addressing workers' shifting values.

Become an 'employer of choice'

With competition in the employment marketplace remaining tough and demand for skilled people outstripping supply, more and more organisations are having to think harder about how to seduce and hold on to talented people who contribute to business success – and also ensure that they are productive.

This has intensified the need for organisations to be recognised as an 'employer of choice' – earning the title 'employer of choice' is not optional, we are told, but necessary in a marketplace driven by the search for competitive success. It can help foster an emotional connection between employees and the organisation, thereby enhancing employee loyalty. A strong employer brand can position a company as an employer of choice and create competitive advantage. Employer branding means ensuring that the employer recognises that it has its own singular identity and culture.

A company faces a daunting challenge in presenting itself as an employer of choice for key talent. We all know that an effective consumer brand is vital to gaining market share and creating customer loyalty. Simply put, your brand is the immediate image, emotion or message that is conjured up when a person thinks of your organisation and its offer. Essentially, the brand building process is just the same in the recruitment market. To formulate a successful brand you have to be clear about the needs, characteristics and expectations of your target employment audience. Which needs do you wish to fulfil? Why should an employee choose you rather than a rival? What sort of offer will both satisfy the needs of your employees and differentiate you from your competitors?

An employer brand is not merely a company name or logo – it's a 'singular identity' that embraces an employee's entire work experience with your organisation. It has to take into account the distinctive mix of transactional and relational returns provided by work and identified with the employing company. An authentic and sustainable employer brand must support organisational values, principles, practices, leadership, culture and behaviour that deliver business results.

When it comes to developing a strong employer brand, clearly financial perks are not the big story here. As the Hay Group (2002) explains:

To become an 'employer of choice' you have to think about the people you employ the same way you think about customers. That means offering them a rewarding environment to work in, not just financial rewards.

In this new business climate, intrinsic rewards – such as quality of leadership, interesting and challenging work, recognition, career advancement and the company brand – are seen by both employees and employers as most important in focusing the workforce on the actions required to achieve strong business results and encourage employees to go beyond the strict boundaries of the job.

In this environment, organisations must mount an extensive marketing campaign to reach out to their target audiences – 'a campaign that will hinge on understanding workforce values and how they influence employee behaviour,' says a report by the Economist Intelligence Unit and HR consultancy Towers Perrin (2001).

Armed with insights into what makes key employees commit to an organisation and involve themselves in the business, companies are in a much better position to articulate the company's value proposition in terms that will engage the target employee groups.

Total reward programmes are distinctive and difficult to copy

With competitive pressures so strong, the need to differentiate reward packages has never been more intense. All too many companies struggling to compete for scarce talent ignore the fact that different things motivate people. Across-the-board policies are not enough: the trick is to cast a wide net and create tailored policies.

> **'Progressive-thinking companies try to create a working environment that not only brings out the best in top performers, but also attracts, nurtures and retains the brightest talent.'**

Rather than imposing standardised packages, the value of total reward programmes lies in creating programmes that are suited to the needs of the organisation and are rooted in an understanding of what optimises employee satisfaction. They encourage employers to look at more imaginative ways to reward their people. They make organisations distinctive.

In the words of Thomas Wilson (2001), a leading US pay consultant:

An integrated reward strategy encourages innovation, not imitation. Companies follow their own path. Consequently their reward systems have given them a unique culture and competitive advantage.

While the design of a pay programme is easily replicated, the way in which total reward programmes are integrated with other practices is often idiosyncratic and linked to organisation-specific factors. Individual practices can be borrowed by rivals, but copying this unique 'organisational personality', as the Hay Group calls it – the positive environment and employment relationship – is much more difficult.

The overwhelming impression to emerge from a recent study by Towers Perrin (1999) is that the days of 'following-the-herd', 'best practice' and importing standard, 'off-the-shelf' pay and benefits 'solutions' are long gone. Quick and easy 'borrowing' of practices from outside, or purchasing of generic evaluation or pay systems, is done on foundations of straw. Such systems subsequently break down in practice, through lack of organisational and cultural 'fit'.

Increased flexibility and choice

Research consistently demonstrates that when people are asked what they value in a reward package, a common response is flexibility and choice (Towers Perrin, 1998). What's more, many individuals have bought into the idea of being treated as clients or customers and have become accustomed to a high level of personal choice. They tell us that they want more choice in benefits to better reflect their lifestyle and state of life.

Gone, then, are the days when HR professionals could take a one-size-fits-all approach to rewards. Progressive-thinking companies are starting to come up with more tailored approaches to stop their brightest staff walking out of the door. Pushed by a desire to create a culture of greater employee responsibility, and at the same time improve employee appreciation of the value of the reward package, companies have increasingly been adopting a much more complex, modern structure of benefits within the context of their overall total reward strategies, designed to meet employee needs.

The trend is for employers to offer a more diverse array of rewards and they are introducing a more flexible approach to provision in an attempt to attract and retain the talent they need. Employers have had to start creating different blends of reward packages for different workforce segments.

Sandra O'Neal (1998) argues that a total rewards approach – which combines transactional and relational rewards – offers tremendous flexibility because it allows awards to be mixed and remixed to meet the different emotional and motivational needs of employees.

Cost is not a problem

One of the key attractions of total reward is its cost efficiency, according to WorldatWork. By remixing their rewards in a more cost-effective way, organisations can strengthen their employees' appreciation, awareness and understanding of the total package without necessarily increasing their overall spend. Towers Perrin also reckons it is largely a matter of reallocating dollars – rather than finding more dollars.

A final word

As companies discover the power of targeted reallocation of rewards and begin to promote the total value of their programmes, they are abandoning the practice of setting pay, benefits and other budgets in isolation, without reference to broad strategic and cost objectives.

WorldatWork (2000)

Table 4 | Advantages of total rewards approach

Increased flexibility	◘ The availability of programmes considered to be part of the work experience may reduce the compensation needed to attract talent, since focus is on 'the whole rewards package'. (Note: compensation savings should not be the driving force behind total rewards.)
◘ The mix of total rewards can be tailored to specific challenges.	
◘ Unique consideration can be given to various job types, geographic locations and demographic issues.	◘ Highly rated companies generally offer competitive programmes within the work experience, besides competitive compensation.
Improved recruitment and retention	**Heightened visibility in a tight labour market**
◘ Highly-rated employers receive more applications.	◘ Strategically designed rewards help organisations attract critical talent from a shrinking labour pool.
◘ Employers can use total rewards as a recruitment tool by presenting the 'total value' of the employment package.	
◘ When employees choose to stay, costs associated with turnover can be reduced.	◘ Offering what employees value can help traditional companies stop the exodus of employees to the emerging companies.
◘ Lower turnover results in lower recruiting costs.	
Reduced labour costs	**Enhanced profitability**
◘ Many elements making up the work experience are low-cost solutions used to attract and retain employees.	◘ A direct link exists between employee motivation and product/service quality.
	◘ Companies rated highly by employees often translate ratings into higher profits.

Source: WorldatWork (2000).

- The switch to a total reward strategy is a huge undertaking for an organisation. Inertia is one of the major obstacles.

- A 'cafeteria' approach to benefits is greatly appreciated by employees, as is reflected in easier recruitment and lower rates of staff turnover.

9 | Case studies

It is the job of leaders to exercise both the judgement and the courage necessary to break with common practice. Those who do will develop organisations in which pay practices actually contribute rather than detract from building high-performance management systems. Those who are stuck in the past are probably doomed to endless tinkering with pay; at the end of the day, they won't have accomplished much, but they will have expended a lot of time and money doing it.

Jeffrey Pfeffer (1998b)

Total reward is a fairly new idea and one that UK employers are only tentatively beginning to explore. So there are relatively few actual examples of the challenges faced by organisations in designing and implementing a total reward programme. Nevertheless, innovation is being made, and a body of knowledge is growing year by year. Below, we learn first-hand from the practical experience of two pioneering organisations in the total reward field, the Financial Services Authority and AstraZeneca.

These case histories offer a unique insight into how organisations are experimenting with total reward solutions to respond to the sort of demanding business challenges facing many of us:

◻ intense competition for labour

◻ major business change – in the case of both the FSA and AstraZeneca, a complicated merger situation

◻ changing employee values and expectations

◻ accelerating global economic development.

> **'...there are few conventions regarding the design of total reward schemes...'**

Why does addressing business problems through a total reward strategy make sense? How then does one craft a total reward strategy? What does the total reward equation allow the organisation to do? The case studies illustrate how two very different organisations have addressed all aspects of rewards to achieve organisational results and at the same time manage costs.

Aside from the need to link a broad package of rewards to corporate cultures and objectives in a way that optimises employee satisfaction, there are few conventions regarding the design of total reward schemes, as our case studies illustrate.

Case study 1:

The Financial Services Authority

www.fsa.gov.uk

Employees: 2,300, all UK-based

Location: Main site in London, one office in Edinburgh

Business activities: The Financial Services Authority (FSA) is an independent non-governmental body, given statutory powers by the Financial Services and Markets Act 2000. It is a not-for-profit company financed by levies on the financial services industry.

Background

In May 1997, Gordon Brown, the Chancellor of the Exchequer, announced a wide-ranging reform of financial services regulation in the UK and the creation of a single regulator. The first stage of the reform was completed a year later when five existing regulatory bodies were brought together. A total of 11 organisations, including the Personal Investment Authority, the Securities and Futures Authority and the Building Societies Commission, were merged over three years.

The groups inherited by the FSA were extremely diverse – some were in the private sector, others were civil servants – with a huge array of terms and conditions.

Reward goals

- Establish a common framework for the transferred groups, including harmonised terms.

- Recruit and retain high-calibre staff.

- Set market-based salaries and ensure that salaries are competitive.

- Develop a single reward package which must be flexible enough to attract and retain a diverse workforce, accommodate different contracts and encapsulate personal choices.

- Reward delivery, performance and personal development – not 'activity' or skills alone.

- Link incentives to business goals and performance against clearly defined objectives.

The programme

The four elements of the FSA's total reward model are:

Pay

Basic salary structured into broad overlapping pay bands, allowing flexibility to reflect the external (financial services and professional) market, plus variable pay in the form of a bonus worth up to 15 per cent of base salary.

Benefits

Core benefits plus a flexible benefits plan, covering pensions, healthcare, insurance, holidays, childcare. Individual employees are given a core benefits package together with a benefits allowance equal to the average cost of a benefits package in the financial services industry, adjusted for age, salary and job level.

Employees may use all this plus up to 10 per cent of salary on benefits, or take all of it in cash, or any point in between.

Learning and development

A career development and learning framework based on competencies, training and secondment opportunities, performance management, induction programme and study sponsorship – including time off and fees paid for relevant study.

Work environment

A single-status climate with open-plan offices and first names for all, an open internal job market, an emphasis on leadership, flat structures and devolved decision-making, a staff consultation committee and work-life balance. A subsidised gym and restaurant are available on site.

Lessons learnt

- Gain buy-in and commitment at all levels to the changes.

- Communicating such major changes is time-consuming and cannot be hurried.

- There was much suspicion about the flex plan – 'Where's the catch?' employees asked.

- Line managers were uneasy about consequences of changes to ways of working.

- Setting robust objectives and measuring performance against them is difficult in a knowledge-based organisation.

- Pay differentials are vast within the various sectors in the financial services market, so trying to develop a common reward package is problematic.

Verdict

The FSA considers that the new total reward package has been a great success:

- As many as 99 per cent of staff transferred to the new contracts.

- Costs were reduced without cutting benefits.

- Labour turnover is currently running at 6 per cent, well below the industry average and 1,600 new recruits have joined the organisation in the three years since the FSA was set up.

- Flexible benefits have proved very popular with both existing staff and new recruits.

- Increased flexibility in the deal has helped the FSA to meet its objective of attracting and retaining a diverse workforce.

Case study 2:

AstraZeneca

www.astrazeneca.com

Employees: 10,500 in UK (50,000 in 100 countries worldwide)

Location: Worldwide operations with corporate headquarters in London

Business activities: One of the world's leading pharmaceutical companies

Background

The challenges facing AstraZeneca are pretty familiar: new legislation, an increasingly competitive marketplace for talent, the pressures of global economies, and a shift in employee expectations in today's society. Its decision to introduce total reward was, like that of the FSA, prompted by a merger situation in 1999, that of two companies Astra AB of Sweden and the UK's Zeneca Group, formerly part of ICI.

The brief given to the human resources department by the company's chief executive was that the two organisations' collection of employment conditions were to be brought together quickly, in an 'industry-leading way' that protected 'legacy' entitlements and at 'minimal cost'.

AstraZeneca's HR team decided a flexible benefits programme was the best solution to integrating the various terms and conditions. It then widened the concept to embrace total reward as the basis of a global

'employment brand', which the company hoped would ultimately help push the business ahead of rivals and retain its best people.

Reward goals

◻ Ensure that everyone benefits from a common reward programme with the same features.

◻ Draw upon the widest possible pool of talent and be an 'employer of choice' for people already employed within the company, as well as for potential new recruits.

◻ Meet varied and changing employee needs by introducing more value, choice and flexibility.

◻ Win the 'war for talent' by being the first in the industry to offer this level of choice and personalisation.

◻ Promote a culture that values, recognises and rewards outstanding performance.

◻ Enhance employees' commitment to AstraZeneca's objectives so that they deliver their personal best.

The programme

The total reward strategy consists of three strands: competitive and flexible reward; excellent development opportunities; and energised working environment. 'These need to be packaged as a single-value proposition, packaged in the minds of employees and potential employees so that the collective value is enhanced beyond the individual value of the components. This takes HR into areas of branding and marketing that are not traditional strengths of our function,' says Malcolm Hurrell, Vice-president of Human Resources at AstraZeneca.

Competitive and flexible reward

At the heart of the compensation component of total reward is the flexible benefits plan, entitled 'Advantage'. This allocates employees a sum equal to their previous salary and benefits package. They can take most of this fund in cash, apart from a small core of benefits – such as a minimum of 22 days' holiday entitlement – or choose to spend it on items from a large menu of existing and new benefits.

The flex menu includes nine 'lifestyle' options (for example, additional holiday, company car, computer, childcare and retail vouchers); two 'health' options (private healthcare); three 'financial' options (pension and financial planning); and four 'protection' options (personal accident, additional life assurance).

Additionally, the compensation package also includes a broadbanded salary structure and three employee share schemes – a performance-based share plan, an Inland Revenue-approved SAYE scheme, and a new Partnership Share Scheme, to be introduced shortly.

Excellent development opportunities

This second pillar of total reward has at its heart the development of an 'active' performance management culture – in other words, not just an annual appraisal but

a management style that coaches, challenges and develops people on the job. Staff are being set stretch performance targets, and the opportunities for learning and progression are increasingly being made clear.

This component of the total reward strategy also encompasses management planning, on-the-job learning, mentoring, e-learning and further education.

Energised working environment

The third and final pillar of total reward is made up of six elements which, if 'executed right', can create a working environment in which people feel motivated and excited. It involves establishing a 'consistent organisation climate' and values to which staff can 'align their personal beliefs and values'.

Effective leadership, communications, the physical environment, recognition by peers as well as managers, and formalised work-life policies are the other important aspects of such an environment.

Lessons learnt

- ◘ AstraZeneca worked closely with Hewitt Associates, a benefits consultancy, throughout the whole process, and thoroughly recommends working with an expert partner in this way.

- ◘ Such difficult projects should be rolled out in phases – AstraZeneca began with 'awareness' for six months, followed by 'engagement' for three months, and then 'enrolment' for a further three months, with the embedding of the new policy by the end of the year.

- Communication campaigns must be tailored to meet the different audiences in the organisation – everyone from the CEO, shopfloor employees, the HR department and trade unions.

- There is a need for 'dedicated project resource'.

- Recognise the broader organisational and policy impact of introducing total reward strategies. 'They impact almost everything,' says Malcolm Hurrell.

Verdict

AstraZeneca considers that its total reward strategy has been very successful in making the merger between the two companies work in the UK:

- 'Advantage' has changed the nature of the employment relationship – staff now have to understand and take personal responsibility for their own benefits choices. This requires an 'adult-to-adult' relationship between the company and the employee, rather than the ICI-style 'parent-child' relationship.

- Nine in ten staff changed their benefits choices when they were given the opportunity to do so.

- Each individual component complements rather than competes with other elements of the reward package.

- AstraZeneca is in little doubt that it is now becoming recognised as an 'employer of choice'.

- Its highly flexible package has helped foster a very strong and 'industry-leading' HR brand conveying 'value, choice and flexibility'.

- The merging of terms and conditions to create 'Advantage' added value to employees' reward package at a minimal integration cost: around 2 to 3 per cent of payroll.

A final word

Employees have told us what they value, and from that we have created a 'total reward' philosophy. However, we are not unique in recognising this deal and this is not rocket science. The key to our success is in helping the organisation fully recognise all the elements as reward and continue to execute the programme better than our competitors in a way that is highly valued by our people.

Malcolm Hurrell, Vice-President Human Resources UK, AstraZeneca

- In only a few years, total reward strategy has become the 'hot topic' in HR.

- Organisations that have introduced a total reward strategy (largely because of external pressures) have reported great benefits for both the employer and employees, with no discernible downside.

10 | Conclusion

It is going to become increasingly important to think through what sort of employment relationship you need to create in your organisation, and how reward policies and practices can build and further that relationship. Incorporating the totality of this relationship, and the employee perspective on it, are going to be vital ingredients in effective reward strategies in the future.

Duncan Brown (2001)

The critical issue for employers today is the way they recruit, reward and retain the most able talent – the people who can make or break the business. The concept of total reward has emerged in recent years as a catch-all phrase to describe the entire premises of how organisations have redefined the way they recognise, reward, recruit and retain employees. Even four years ago, total reward was little heard of in the UK. Now talk of it abounds.

Its supporters argue that managing the entire portfolio of financial and non-financial aspects of reward in a more co-ordinated fashion may encourage more positive employee commitment and loyalty to the organisation and contribute to business success. But to be honest, though, none of this is really new.

This idea that it has never been more important to recognise the importance of aligning the reward strategy with employee values and needs does fit neatly with contemporary thinking in HR management and management theory which says how fundamental people are to business success.

A growing body of research is emerging that clearly demonstrates a relationship between good people practices, high levels of employee commitment and superior business performance (Caulkin 2001). The argument is that there is a demonstrable link between HR and reward practices that promote high levels of job satisfaction and employees' willingness to 'go the extra mile'. So human resource management can – and does – contribute to the bottom line.

Although it is a fundamentally simple concept, nobody should pretend that total reward is not a difficult and time-consuming process to put into practice. Oh, that it would be so easy. If you are looking for a quick-fix solution, forget it. There are no 'three easy steps' to engaging employees' hearts and minds. Companies discover that engaging people in the drive for improved business performance is a long-term change process. It is incredibly complex out there.

Total reward programmes encompass a gargantuan brief, requiring various specialisms in people management and development to be integrated effectively. Total reward strategies are especially daunting to implement, argue Murlis and Watson (2001), because they require managers who are 'willing to work with the thinking that goes with this more comprehensive approach'.

> **'Companies discover that engaging people in the drive for improved business performance is a long-term change process. It is incredibly complex out there.'**

As Professor Jeffrey Pfeffer (1998b) has observed, it is often simpler for managers to tinker with their compensations system than to change an organisation's culture and the way work is organised. What's more, it is 'easier to see what everyone else is doing and then do the same'.

But Pfeffer has a stark warning for those managers who 'follow the crowd': applying off-the-shelf compensation strategies will not push your companies ahead of rivals. Pfeffer thinks that good reward strategies are about customisation and tailoring.

It must certainly be the case that a company cannot earn 'abnormal' returns by following the crowd. That's true about marketplace strategies, and it's true about compensation.

The successful investment in a new total reward package involves a great deal of effort, commitment and expertise. Certainly, no off-the shelf solution is available. Each organisation has unique circumstances that will influence its total rewards decisions. So these programmes are highly idiosyncratic and must be tailored to each employer's individual situation.

While the path to total reward is strewn with difficulties, this should not, however, prevent further exploration of the ideas behind this approach with a view to implementing at least some of its principles when possible. If it were easy to do, it would not be a source of long-term success.

Broadly applicable

It is easy to think that such a clear, comprehensive and strategic approach to reward is a luxury reserved for the global players. Total reward is particularly applicable where retaining intellectual capital and knowledge-based skills is a vital source of long-term success. But the most successful organisations understand the importance of engaging and motivating all their people. Even shopfloor employees and those involved in service delivery are perpetually under pressure to improve quality, keep a lid on costs and reduce process times to meet customers' expectations and keep the organisation ahead of the competition.

Whatever the organisation – manufacturer or service-provider, private or public, for-profit or not-for-profit – the underlying principles at work here are broadly applicable. A central theme of the total reward rhetoric is that the solution for stopping rampant employee turnover and engaging and motivating the workforce begins with a thorough understanding of the problem.

The process is motivational

Total reward requires an integrated approach rooted in an understanding of employee values and the rewards that motivate your people to deliver results. Fortunately it is relatively easy to get the facts. The best way to *begin* such an understanding is through carefully crafted surveys, focus groups and the like. As the Hay Group explains:

You need to collect specific data to identify the most significant needs within the different demographic segments of your workforce. Only then can you develop high-impact programmes to meet employees' needs and effectively engage them. One-size-fits-all no longer works as an HR or reward strategy.

What's more, one essential message emerging from the Hay Group's research is that the process of moving towards total reward is by its very nature – with its emphasis on consultation, involvement and communication – motivational.

So employers would do well to apply one effective technique: all companies need to do is stop and ask their people, listen, let them know their views are important, and then act on the findings. Once you have measured the 'employee motivators' you have some solid facts and figures. Using this agenda for change, you can adjust the elements of your people and reward programmes that will be needed to support future growth accordingly – which may mean refocusing rewards on priority areas for our more diverse workforces.

Question received wisdom

Also take Pfeffer's advice (1998a) and question the received reward wisdom within your business. His contention is that many managers are trapped in unproductive ways of thinking about pay, which they find difficult to escape. The reason is that they are afraid to challenge the myths about compensation and rethink their own assumptions.

Perhaps it is because adjusting reward is easier than remedying basic problems of too much stultifying control and too little meaning or enjoyment in the job. But for whatever the reasons, managers should ignore the many blandishments and the temptation to try to solve most of their organisational problems through pay.

Reward management is ready for reform. This is the only conclusion to be drawn from the growing body of knowledge in the total reward literature. We are urged to abandon the tried and tested ways of thinking about reward. Move from a piecemeal to a more holistic approach. Think about reward more broadly. Look at the bigger picture and redefine how employee rewards can be adapted to support the new landscape of workplace issues.

The critical challenge is determining which rewards will engage and encourage more positive employee commitment among those employees that the organisation has identified as most important to long-term success. While there is little doubt that the extrinsic, financial aspects of reward remain a key element of the new working relationship, they are not on their own sufficient to reinforce desired behaviour or support the kind of performance breakthroughs so many companies seek today. Many of us evidently care about things beyond the purely monetary. Employees may well feel well rewarded but we cannot infer from that that they understand the organisation goals and are committed to helping to achieve them.

That's why the Hay Group (2002) reckons that inspirational leadership is, without doubt, the biggest perk. As the Hay Group puts it:

Would you channel your discretionary effort into your work if you believed that your organisation's leadership was second-rate or that its values were either off-base or ill-defined? You probably wouldn't, regardless of how much money you made, or how good your benefits and other employment conditions were.

By putting less emphasis on financial aspects to retain top talent, companies can appeal to the personal values and lifestyle choices of today's employees. They can begin to create the sort of mutually beneficial employment relationship that will help build the mindset required among employees to direct their efforts to the key strategic priorities of the business.

Total reward has the possibility of being a very powerful management tool that can help to underpin structural and cultural change and support the achievement of business goals. As

companies vie for scarce talent, they could do a lot worse than apply some of the total reward techniques to give them the edge.

A final word

Stars tend to be intrinsically motivated, and they capture most of the 'prizes' on offer – the most interesting work, the best promotions, big salary increases and bonuses. The more difficult challenge for employers is capturing the hearts and minds of good reliable employees who are not stars but who are significantly more productive when engaged.

Hay Group (2002)

References

Brown D. (2001)

Reward strategies: From intent to impact. London, CIPD.

Caulkin S. (2001)

Performance Through People: New People Management. London, CIPD. (The Change Agenda.)

Cox A. and Purcell J. (1998)

'Searching for leverage: pay systems, trust, motivation and commitment in SMEs', in *Trust, Motivation and Commitment*, S. J. Perkins and St John Sandringham (eds). Faringdon, Strategic Remuneration Research Centre.

Economist Intelligence Unit *and* Towers Perrin (2001)

Business, People and Rewards: Surviving and thriving in the new economy. London, Economist Intelligence Unit.

Hay Group (2001)

The Retention Dilemma: Why productive workers leave – seven suggestions for keeping them. London, Hay Group.

Hay Group (2002)

Engage Employees and Boost Performance. London, Hay Group.

Incomes Data Services (2000)

Improving staff retention. London, IDS. (IDS Study 692, July 2000.)

Milkovich G. T. *and* Bloom M. (1998)

'Rethinking international compensation'. *Compensation and Benefits Review*. January/February.

Murlis H. *and* Watson S. (2001)

'Creating employee engagement: Transforming the employment deal'. *Benefits and Compensation International*. Vol. 30, No. 8, April.

O'Neal S. (1998)

'The phenomenon of total rewards'. *ACA Journal*. Vol. 7, No. 3, Autumn.

Pfeffer J. (1998a)

The Human Equation: Building profits by putting people first. Boston, Harvard Business School Press.

Pfeffer J. (1998b)

'Six dangerous myths about pay'. *Harvard Business Review*, May–June.

Thompson M. *and* Heron P. (2001)

Innovation and the Psychological Contract in the Knowledge Business. Oxford, Templeton College.

Towers Perrin (1998)

Benefit Effectiveness Index. London, Towers Perrin.

Towers Perrin (1999)

Euro Rewards 2000: Reward challenges and changes – survey results. London, Tower Perrin.

Tulgan B. (2000)

Managing Generation X: How to bring out the best in young talent. New York, W. W. Norton.

Watson Wyatt (2002)

Strategic Rewards. European survey results. London, Watson Wyatt.

Wilson T. B. (2001)

'Rewards that work'. *Mastering People Management. Part 4. Financial Times,* 5 November.

WorldatWork (2000)

Total Rewards: From strategy to implementation. Scottsdale, Ariz., WorldatWork.

WorldatWork – 14040 N. Northsight Blvd. – Scottsdale, AZ 85260
Direct Line: 1 480/922-2095
E-mail: ajantz@worldatwork.org
WorldatWork
The Professional Association for Compensation, Benefits and Total Rewards

Zingheim P. K. and Schuster J.R. (2000)

Pay People Right! Breakthrough reward strategies to create great companies. San Franciso, Jossey-Bass.